ON HAWAIIAN FOLK MUSIC

Produced by Island Heritage Limited

Directed by Robert B. Goodman

Dedication by Ka'upena Wong

Texts by Samuel Crowningburg-Amalu, Herbert Kawainui Kane,
and Emerson C. Smith

Photographs by Theodore Kelsey

Illustrations by Martin Charlot and Herbert Kawainui Kane

Historical Research by June Gutmannis

Book Design and Typography by Herb Kane

Associate Art Director, Yoshio Hayashi

 AN ISLAND HERITAGE BOOK

ON HAWAIIAN FOLK MUSIC

Produced and published by
Island Heritage Limited, Norfolk Island, Australia

This edition first published in Japan in August 1971

Prime distribution in the Hawaiian Islands, Canada, and the
Continental United States by
W. W. Distributors Ltd.
1132 Auahi Street, Honolulu, Hawaii 96814

Library of Congress Catalog Card Number: 77-173474

Engraving, printing, and binding by
Nissha Printing Co., Kyoto, Japan

Set in 16 point Century Expanded by
Star Bulletin Printing Company
and in Press Roman IBM Composer type by
Associated Journals Hawaii, Inc., Honolulu

Mary Abigail Ka-wena-'ula-o-ka-lani-a-Hi'iaka-i-ka-poli-o-Pele-ka-wahine-'ai-honua Wiggin Pukui is a storehouse of Hawaiian culture. She has been a major source of information on old Hawaiian culture for students, teachers, scientists, old and young, and most importantly for her fellow Hawaiian. As one writer has recorded, "Her motivation is the urgency she feels to research and record all possible knowledge of the indigenous culture of Hawaii." This Kawena has done and continues to do in the fields of ethnology, history, linguistics, sociology and natural history.

Born at Hale-ola, the home of her grandmother, Po'ai, over-looking the town of Na'alehu, Ka'u, Hawaii, she was raised as a punahele child. This meant special attention in her upbringing. Her first nine years were spent with her beloved Po'ai, who exposed her to the ancient lore and rituals of the *kahuna lapa'au* (medical priest), of the priesthood of Lono, and the prayers and dances of Pele. This was the foundation for Kawena's life work.

Of her work to collect, preserve and share the *mele* (chant and "song") of old Hawaii she says, "A lei of flowers will fade and perish. A lei of poetry remains forever fresh." For all who have plucked the "flowers" from Kawena's garden to weave a "lei" of their own, we say thank you dear Kawena.

KA'UPENA WONG
EDDIE KAMAE
MOE KEALE
JOE MARSHALL
GABBY PAHINUI
DAVID ROGERS

SING TO ME THE SONGS THAT I MIGHT HEAR THEM AGAIN

By SAMUEL CROWNINGBURG-AMALU
PHOTOGRAPHS: THEODORE KELSEY

HE came dancing upon the silver waves, his feet lightly tripping over the froth, his flesh glistening with the wild sea spray blowing.

He came with laughter shining in his eyes. Wreathed in golden blossoms, his loins girdled with mountain vines. And in his hair were ferns of the valleys, fragile and fragrant.

HE was Laka, the son of Hina-Manauluae, the goddess of growing things. And of Pili-aoao who came from the wild lands of Hapa-kuela where lie the birth sands of the great Pele. He was Laka, the youth of merriment, the child of music and of the dance. He was the godling child of the gods, born of a goddess and of a man. He was Laka, the golden youth. The forever young, the child of beauty.

AND Laka called upon the ocean, upon the deep waters flowing. Raise up for me the songs of the sea tha I might hear them again and remember in my heart how sing the ocean tides. Out of the very depths of you, raise up for me a song and sing to me. Tell me of the ancient lands that are no more, that have vanished into the deeps of thee. Tell me of the lost shores that are departed from the face of Earth to be seen no more. Tell me who sleep in the dark bosom of thee.

SING to me of the breast of ocean, of the spume of the great whale, of the flashing trails of the shark. Tell me of the monsters that haunt your dark valleys and the chasms

of thee. Tell me of the far distant sands where lap your wavelets in soft whispers. Or where you crash upon the rocks in thunderous roar. Tell me how the moonlight spreads its cloak of silver upon thee. How out of the greying dawn, the first golden ray of sunlight kisses your lips to waken you to the day. Tell me how scarlet burns the evening sun upon the ocean deeps.

AND Laka stepped out of the ocean, out of the sea. And he stood alone upon the shore. He raised his eyes to the hills, and he called to the glory of Earth.

O, THOU who art the child of Papa and upon whom hath fallen the fertile rays of Wakea. O, you highlands and you lowlands. You deep valleys, you crested mountain heights. O, you broad plains and you hillocks covered with verdure. Sing ye all to me of Earth. Tell me of her birth in the infant hours of this universe, when this sun was new born in the heavens. Tell me of the fires that burn in her bosom, of the flames that rise out of her to scorch and sear the many lands. Tell me of her fury in the hours of her wrath, of her storms that ravage her shorelines, of her mighty winds and of her pounding rains. Yea, sing to me too of her gentleness, of the

sweetness of her waters, and the richness of her great bounty.

TELL me how twines the maile on the boughs of trees, how blooms the soft 'ilima, how fall the tender petals of the lehua. Tell me where the dragons lie. Tell me where the owls fly. For these are sacred to me and to my house.

AND pluck for me the mountain ferns. And weave them into a garland for my wearing. That I might enter into thy house, O Earth, and into thy halls to bless thy maidens who shall come before me unravished and intact. That I might bless the sons of thee, O Earth, who come before me as virgins. Innocent in their unknowing. For I am Laka. And the virgins of the land, sons and daughters alike, are sacred to me. Let them not come to me defiled. Lest I turn from them. And from thee, O Earth. Lest I turn from thee and know thee no more. Nor the sons of thee. Nor thy daughters.

LET the virgins come to me from over all the many lands, and I will know them who are my very own.

AND Laka moved further into the land. He walked deep into the dark valleys. He bathed his flesh in the cataracts falling. He rose to

the high mountain tops and stood amid the fields of snow. He surveyed the land and the many islands. And he blessed them saying:

O, THOU gracious land of Wakea, born of the night and nutured by the endless sea. Thou great islands that rose out of the bosom of Earth, out of the cauldron of fire, out of the flames that burn forever in the breast of Earth. Thou art the children of the Maiden Papa. Of Papa who came from Healani, that distant world now lost among the stars. Of Papa who bared her womb to the sun and brought forth young.

AND thou art the children of Wakea. Of Wakea who came upon Papa the Maiden. Who loved her. Who ravished the beauty of her. Who came in all his glory upon the breast of Earth and made fertile her fields and brought life unto her seas.

THEN Laka raised his arms unto the many islands and he blessed each of them saying:

O HAWAII, great land of Keawe. Of Keawe who was mighty among the warriors and great among the princes. Of Keawe who raised high his ensigns and his banners that all must fall down before them and worship him who was lord over all the land. To thee,

Hawaii, I give the scarlet lehua and entwine them in the fragrant leaves of Panaewa.

O MAUI of Kamalalawalu and Pi'ilani. Ye are indeed the sons of battle. I have walked over the snows of Haleakala and I have kissed the finger tips of Lilinoe. I have worn upon my own shoulders the golden robes of Pi'ilani. Of Pi'ilani who brought peace to thee. Of Pi'ilani who brought riches forth out of the land. To thee, I give the rose for thy wearing and the first faint blush of the early dawn.

OAHU, child of beauty and mother of the stranger. Oahu of Kakuhihewa, the Lord. Of Kakuhihewa who bore in his hand the silver wand. Of Kakuhihewa who was the fairest lord in all the many islands. O for the Plains of Mamala and the broad lands of Lele. The ranges of the Ko'olau and of Waianae. To thee, I give the soft 'ilima, golden and tender as the brush of a butterfly's wing. To thee, Oahu, my fairest daughter.

O KAUAI, sacred land of Mano, Lord of the Night. Of Mano born of the silken mats. Of Mano in whose veins flowed the bloods of Ahukini and of La'a. Of La'a who came from Kahiki. To thee are forever sacred the pungent seed of the mokihana. And to thee, to

thee O beauteous land, are holy the leaves of makana, the fern leaves of the laua'e.

O MOLOKAI, grey Moloka'i, holy Moloka'i where have been reared the great temples of the Kaula. Thy lands are sacred to Lono, Lord of the East. The same who rose out of the loins of him who was the Prince of Mischief, of Kaulula'au. To thee I give the white blossom of the kukui, the seed that beareth light into the darkness. Thy lands are holy, O Moloka'i. Thy valleys are sacred. They are inviolate. Let none desecrate them forever.

O LANAI, Land of Exiles. Thy red hills are damp with the tears of the wretched. Thy shorelines are burnt with the orange strings of the kaunaoa. O Ni'ihau of Kiha, the first born of Papa and of Wakea. To thee are given the shells along thy beaches and on thy shores. And beloved Kaho'olawe, child of the sea. To thee the hinahina, grey as thy rocks are grey and thriving upon the very air itself as thou must also.

O THOU many islands that sail the breast of ocean, of these great waters that are the Sea of Kanaloa. Of Kanaloa who is the god, the

brother of Kane and of Ku. Of Kanaloa who sustaineth life. O Thou Islands of Hawai'i, sing to me. Sing to me.

AND when Laka was done, he sat in silence and brooded over the days that were to come. He looked upon the morrows that were to come. He looked upon the distant dawns that had not as yet arisen out of the sea. He looked upon them and he wept.

O, my beloved land, my golden islands. There will come first upon thee the children of Kamene, they who will be remembered as the Menehune. And they will bless the land with their industry and the peaceful tenor of their days. And then will come the Wa, who are bred of battle, who are cursed, who have been defiled so that their blood is no more sweet unto the gods. And they will pillage the haunts of the Menehune so that the little ones will go forth over the seas to seek aid and succour. And they will come upon the Lords of the Kena, the same who came first upon Earth from the burning worlds of Healani. And the Kena will come to the aid of the Menehune, and they will come in their myriads to drive away the Wa and to slaughter them where they stand.

ᗅᑎᗞ the Kena will raise up their own gods and erect their own sanctuaries. They will reign as masters of the land. Their princes will walk as gods over the hills, and there will be none to stand before them as equals. Yea, and the Kena will quarrel among themselves and raise up great armies to wage war against each other. And they will affright the land, and the blood of princes will flow over Earth. There will come fear to mar the beauty of these islets, and man will no more walk in peace.

AND the Kena will rise up and devastate the land. They will not know any peace. Neither in the lands that they will rule nor even among themselves. And their princes will cast down their gods, the very gods that raised them up will they cast down. They will tear down their holy temples and defile their sacred places. And they shall be lost and cast away in turn.

THEN out of the seas, the great seas, will come a host of strangers. And they will change the

face of the land until the Kena themselves will walk as strangers in their own homelands. And the Kena will weep. They will gnash their teeth. They will cry out for succour. But there shall be none. No, not until there cometh to them a prince out of the north who will call upon them once more to rise. And the Kena will hear the call of their prince, and they will gather to him. And they who are the Kena will stand up again in these lands as princes thereof. And so will they remain until all time is done.

SO sang Laka as he sat on the hill that is called Pu'uhonua, the hill of Earth. So did he sing, and so has it come to pass. So did they come who were first upon these Islands, the Menehune. The little ones who made fertile the many lands. And then in their own turn came the Wa who ravaged the land and made great war among the Menehune. And then followed the Kena who waxed mighty over all of Hawai'i. And the Kena cast down their gods and were in turn cast down. And strangers from out of the sea came to rule the land and to carve alien images over all the hills and the valleys of Hawai'i.

THIS is the story of Hawai'i. And out of this tale arose the songs and music of our people.

WAIPIO

Story and Illustrations by
HERBERT KAWAINUI KANE

"To understand the old Hawaiians, you must listen to their music," my father said. "I know at least fifty Hawaiian songs about love or the beauty of certain places, but only one song about war."

His once-strong singing voice was now a whisper. He was too weak to accompany me on one last trip back to Hawaii. We sat in the darkening room, looking out at the falling snow and the bleak winter landscape.

I had brought my tapes of Hawaiian folk music to his house in the little Wisconsin town where he had met my mother fifty years ago. He sat in his favorite chair, his old ukulele on his lap, staring out at the blowing snow. But I knew that he was seeing the sunlit green of Waipio Valley, his birthplace on the island of Hawaii. His mind was filled with boyhood memories, little vignettes of his life in that remote place, so many years ago. On the tape, Gabby Pahinui, Eddie Kamae, and the Sons of Hawaii were singing "Ulili E," the song to the sandpiper. Listening to the rhythms, you could see the little piping shorebird prancing along the water's edge where the surf swirls up on the wet sand.

"I remember when I first heard that song in Waipio Valley," Dad mused. "One day someone came whipping a mule into the village, telling everyone that a famous musician who had been visiting in Kukuihaele was about to come down the cliff trail into Waipio. I can't recall the musician's name . . . I was just a small boy then, and it was so long ago.

"All our women got busy preparing food, and the young girls who weren't minding babies were called to help. We boys—myself, Solomon Kala, John Thomas, Bill Kualii, and Ah Wo—ran to the pali and started up the long trail— up that thousand-foot cliff, like mountain goats." His eyes glistened with pleasure at the memory.

"Before we reached the top, we could hear shouts of laughter from the party coming down. We met them at the topmost bend, where the trail starts down the side of the cliff. That's where I met the writer, Jack London, and his wahine one evening about ten years later.

"I knew who the musician was right away, because he was the only stranger. The others were all from Kukuihaele, as far as I could tell, and they were talking and laughing and having good fun. One was carrying what appeared to be the stranger's guitar and ukulele, and there was some other gear in a rice sack slung from the pommel of one of the mule saddles.

"They were all on mules. Someone made a joke about the possibility of going off the narrow trail and falling a thousand feet down the cliff. Someone else said, 'Don't take the bottle with you!' and everyone laughed and laughed. Horses have enough sense to stay close to the cliff wall, but they didn't have any horses and you know how those damn mules always walk right on the edge.

"Son, do you remember how long that trail seemed? On the way down the stranger would stop and ask about something that had caught his eye in the valley, pointing to the beach or to one of the waterfalls. He talked to us about how much work it must have been for the ancient Hawaiians to cut the trail out of the cliff with stone adzes. That was a new thought to me, something I had never considered. And when the twin waterfalls of Hiilawe came into view at the last turn in the trail, the stranger couldn't take his eyes from the sight. For him, Waipio was a unique and beautiful place.

"As we reached the village, everyone gathered around—shy but eager to be friendly. The stranger was first introduced to all the old folks. Mutual friendships and distant family relationships were explored to everyone's satisfaction. Invitations were offered with elaborate casualness, received with a nod of the head and a smile, as the stranger pretended to be busy tuning his guitar.

"His was not the heroic figure I had expected. When he dismounted he looked short alongside the people of our valley, and I was startled to see that one leg was crippled. But that night when the music started at the Thomas place, when I first heard his voice and his guitar, I knew why he was famous.

"We boys crowded around the bottom of the steps, and in the glow of kerosene lanterns we could see the visitor sitting up on the veranda. The local musicians clustered around him, each with a guitar or ukulele. Behind them, the old folks sat on chairs. Out in the darkness, the yard was soon filled with people.

"It was a magic moment. I had never known that a guitar could sound like that. And his voice! Whenever I hear Gabby's voice on your tapes, I think of that voice I heard so long ago. When he sang, every rock and tree in the valley seemed to be listening.

"You remember how Sam Lia became the songwriter for Waipio after his father died? He must be eighty-five by now and still writes me in the flowery old Hawaiian. Give him my best aloha when you go back there! You know, it was Sam Lia's father who wrote "Hiilawe," even though someone else later took the credit for it."

My father turned to look at me then, and his voice grew stronger.

"Say, don't you believe those who say that folk songs just happen. These songs may get worked on by others along the way, but every one of them was originated by someone. You know David Makaoi, the Japanese orphan who was raised by a Hawaiian family in Waipio? He wrote, a while back, that somebody is going around copywriting Hawaiian folk songs. Auwe! Dirty shame. The people who wrote those songs may be dead and forgotten now, but those songs were their gift to Hawaii. That was all they had to give. If what Makaoi says is true, then some of our boys should throw that greedy buggah to the sharks, bimeby."

A song by Genoa Keawe was on the tape now, her brilliant voice trilling like birdsong in an enchanted forest. A song about a sweetheart. Dad listened for a while, then went on talking about Waipio.

He described the effect of the stranger's visit. Every day a crowd of loafers gathered in front of the Chinese store, softly strumming their ukes and guitars, frequently bursting into boisterous song. Everyone who could lay their hands on an instrument suddenly became a musician. The stranger's techniques were studied and practiced. And every night an impromptu concert formed around him on someone's veranda.

In the midst of all this easygoing exchange, two couples decided to get married. Immediately, preparations for a big luau were made. Everyone contributed food, including my father and the other boys, who scrambled among the rocks out in the surf picking the tasty little shellfish, opihi. Others netted mullet in the old fishponds, or climbed the cliffs to catch fresh water shrimp in the high pools that interrupt some of the waterfalls. Fires blazed in the ground ovens, and pigs, chickens and delicacies prepared and wrapped in ti leaves were roasted on the red-hot stones. The Chinese brought food also, and barbecued a pig in their own way. Throughout three days of festivities, the okolehao flowed like water—all provided by the "ti root boys" from their stills in the back of the valley.

The stranger sang for both weddings. One was held at the Congregational Church, where they had a bell; the other at the Mormon Church, where the flock was called to worship by the blowing of a conch shell. At the luau, the stranger sang a new song he had composed, in which—to everyone's immense delight—there was a most indirect and discreet reference to the fact that one of the grooms had another wife in Laupahoehoe.

The wedding party went on for three days of eating, drinking, laughing, fighting, lovemaking, and singing—always singing. At the end a whole beef was strung up, prominently displayed, and everyone took some home.

When the stranger left the valley, his new friends escorted him all the way to Honokaa.

"I ran along behind them," my father recalled, "following them up the pali trail until Sam Lia let me ride behind him on the rump of his horse. Outside of Kukuihaele, just before they made me go back, we apssed a group of Japanese working on an irrigation system in the sugar fields. They were strangers to Hawaii. We couldn't speak with them, so we stared at them, and they stared at us. Then someone struck a chord on a guitar and just for the hell of it we gave them a song. You should have seen the amazement on their faces, breaking into grins at the serenade. Some of them even waved to us.

"You know, son, back in those days musicians could wander about and be welcome everywhere. If they needed clothes or tobacco or the loan of a horse, these were provided—for they always gave more than they received.

And before they left, as a final gift, they might compose a song about the beauty of the area, or invent a merry hula about a local scandal that had all the tongues wagging. Or perhaps their gift was just a slack-key tune about one of the local beauties riding by on a galloping horse, her long pa'u skirt whipping in the breeze." That, according to my father, was the way so many songs came to be written about the beauty of certain places, or about love—sacred or profane. It was dark outside now, a cold, snowy night. Dad stared out of the window, silent for a long time, searching the corners of his memory for something he must not forget to tell me. Without speaking of it, we both knew that—as with so many of the old Hawaiians—the premonition of his going was upon him. On the tape recorder Ed Kenney's voice filled the room, setting fire to a great old song. Then the warm and vibrant voice of Marlene Sai.

And then Gabby's voice was on the tape again
rising over a magical slack-key guitar.
"Nobody can learn to sing like that in a music
school," my father said. "That kind voice
takes plenty time and plenty trouble."
He fell silent, his fingers gently touching the
battered ukulele on his lap. The snow had
stopped and the moon was breaking through
the clouds. For a long time he was silent.
The Sons of Hawaii were all singing
harmony, now.
"When I was a boy, I heard an old man
say that the Hawaiian gods died because
there were no priests left to keep them alive,"
he said softly. "And if it were not for a few
people like those boys and the others we've
been listening to, our music would be dead
too. "Gabby's kids—Hawaii's kids—good thing
that they're picking it up. That's one part
of Hawaii that no sonofabitch can ever take
away from them."

OHE KA'EKE (*Bamboo Tubes)*
"In their regular concerts, each man had a bamboo, which was of a different length, and gave a different tone; these they beat against the ground, and each performer, assisted by the note given by this instrument, repeated the same note, accompanying it by words, by which means it was rendered sometimes short and sometimes long. In this manner, they sang in chorus, and not only produced octaves, but fell on disagreeable to the ear. . . ."
CAPTAIN JAMES KING 1778-1779

ON HAWAIIAN FOLK MUSIC

TEXT by EMERSON C. SMITH
ILLUSTRATIONS by MARTIN CHARLOT

Of all the many stories about Hawaii, none is more amazing than the story of how Hawaii's music grew from ancient chants to folk songs in less than a hundred years.

Hawaiian folk music, as we know it today, is a youthful art. It is based on highly sophisticated chants that were developed over several thousand years. The ancient Hawaiian songs were called *mele,* and were really poems which were chanted, often accompanied by rhythm instruments and by dances called *hula.* These *mele* were of great importance to the Hawaiian people, for in them they preserved their legends, traditions, genealogies, and history. The *mele* and *hula* were also part of their religion, and through them they paid homage to *Laka,* as well as *Lono, Kane, Kanaloa, Ku,* and to many lesser gods, such as *Pele, Hi'iaka,* and *Kamapua'a.* The same thing happened in Europe during the middle ages where minstrels, troubadours, and minnesingers preserved the legends and history of the time in song.

It is axiomatic that the oldest history of every nation is found in its folk songs, its nursery rhymes, and its chants. The chants of Hawaii are excellent examples of how a people can preserve their ancient lore for an incredibly long time. All people have legends relating to dragons, and the Hawaiians were no exception, though their dragons were beneficent creatures called *mo'o.* All nations have a legend of a great flood, which the Hawaiian people know as the *Sea of Ka-hinali'i.* All nations have a remembrance of the sun

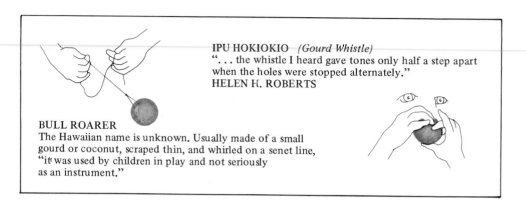

standing still, as recorded in Joshua 10:13 and in Isaiah 38:8. The Hawaiian people have a similar legend, which tells how *Maui* lassoed the sun and held it until his mother's *kapa* dried. Many of you know of the *Kumulipo,* a 2102-line Hawaiian creation chant composed about 1700 A.D. Its first four lines translate to:

> At the time when the Earth became hot,
> At the time when the heavens turned about,
> At the time when the sun was darkened
> To cause the moon to shine.

Parallel passages found in the legends of many other lands describe an event which some believe was a world-wide catastrophe that occurred in 687 B.C.

For every epic poem of the stature of the *Kumulipo* there were thousands of lesser *mele* of every sort: *mele oli* for narratives, *mele inoa* to recite the genealogy or achievements of a person, *mele wehi* to honor a person, *mele kanikau* or dirges, *mele aupuni* or national anthems, *mele paikau* for marching, *mele ka'i kaua* or war chants, *mele haipule* or religious chants, *mele kahea* requesting permission to enter, *mele ka'i* sung when dancers enter,

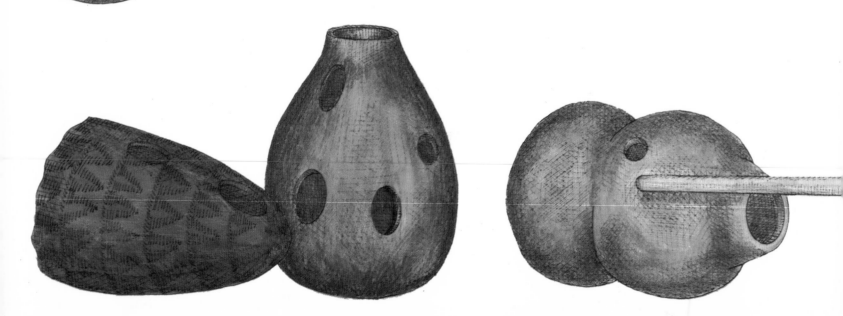

mele kuahu sung before the hula school altar, *mele kaʻi hoʻi* sung when the dancers leave, *mele hoʻonana* to soothe children, *mele hoʻohiamoe* to induce sleep, *mele hoʻala* to wake a child, *mele hoʻoipipo* for wooing, and *mele hula* to accompany dancing. Truly, there were *mele* for every possible occasion!

To the ancient Hawaiian, the chief charm of the singing lay in the words, and the tune was thought to be unimportant. Therefore only rhythm instruments, such as the *pahu* or drum, the *ipu* or gourd, the *ʻuliʻuli* or gourd rattle, the *ʻiliʻili* or pebble castenets, the *puʻili* or split bamboo, and the *kalaʻau* or resonant sticks were used for accompaniment. The dancers wore anklets of teeth called *kupeʻe* which added their rhythmic clicking. The primitive nature of this accompaniment is proof that the Hawaiians left their traditional home in *Hawaiki* before they were exposed to the influences which moulded the music of the Egyptians, Hebrews, Hindus, and Chinese. Some students infer, solely from the evidence of the complex rhythms and primitive melodies of their music, that they left the Asiatic mainland not later than 1000 B.C.

We know that rhythm preceded melody, and that the earlier rhythms were more complex and continually shifting in pattern. Some Asiatic music has this "shifting rhythms" characteristic even today. It would be arrogant to call these irregular rhythms primitive, and one might even speculate that these rhythms are more sophisticated than our own. Possibly the chief reason we use regular, recurring rhythms is because we depend on reading them in musical notation from a piece of paper. It is very difficult, even for a trained musician, to transcribe a rhythm which changes its pattern (its time signature) continuously. The first *ha'ole* (white persons) who tried to transcribe Hawaiian chants and songs were confused by the changing rhythms and tried to interpret them in terms of a single time signature. We can see evidence of this in early song collections, where many songs are only 13, 14, or 15 measures long, instead of the natural 16 measures.

The ancient melodies were primitive. The Hawaiians had no scales, in the sense we think of scales. Their chanting was on a few tones, usually only two or three, but when the chanter had chosen the tones to be used they were used faithfully throughout the chant. If one is willing to say that the repeated use of a selected small group of tones establishes a scale, then the Hawaiian people used a large number of scales. All the people of the Orient have the ability to hear, use, and enjoy very small tone intervals, and the use of small tone intervals was a characteristic of the ancient Hawaiian chants. If we define a "half-tone" as a minor second, you will then understand when we say that ancient Hawaiian music used intervals as small as "quarter-tones."

We know that the ancestors of the Hawaiians were Caucasians. We know too that these master seamen navigated by the stars and were able to retrace their path if necessary. The Hawaiian language today retains the names of five planets, nine constellations, and eighty-one stars which they knew. The stick charts of island groups which some Polynesians used were marvels of accuracy compared with Roman maps of the same period. We know, too, that these bold men were sailing eighty-foot double canoes carrying sixty passengers out on the broad Pacific about a thousand years before Leif Ericcson made the first Atlantic crossing to North America in 1003 A.D. Probably several centuries passed before their island-hopping took them the long path through Indonesia, and the Caroline, Marshall, and Phoenix islands to *Ra'iatea* in the Society Islands. One can imagine the joy of these voyagers, whose ancestors had eked out a meagre existence on coral atolls, when they first saw the cloud-piercing mountains, the lush valleys, and the full-running streams of *Ra'iatea.* Soon they discovered *Tahiti,* larger and equally fertile, only a hundred miles away.

Tahitian legends tell us that *Hawai'i-loa* and his navigator *Makali'i* were the first to make the 2400-mile voyage from Tahiti to Hawaii about 450 A.D., and that they returned to Tahiti for their families. The *ali'i* or chiefs who commanded these canoes and the *ho'okele wa'a* who navigated them were superior, educated men.

When the first *ali'i* arrived in Hawaii they found the islands inhabited by a race of people called *menehune. The menehune* may have arrived by accident in canoes blown off their course by storms, for they had brought no food plants or animals with them, and were living on *hala* fruit, *ti* roots, and *'ohelo* berries. Archeologic research indicates that the *menehune* moved on to *Kaua'i, Nihoa,* and Necker Islands, then vanished completely. If they had *mele* telling of their history, these too vanished.

Between the Hawaiian islands of *Maui* and *Kaho'olawe* is a channel called *Ke-ala-i-kahiki* (the way to Tahiti), a present-day reminder of the many round trips made between 450 and 1275 A.D. which inspired *mele* like this:

> *'Eia na wa'a, kau mai;*
> Here are the canoes, get aboard;
>
> *E ho'i e noho ia Hawai'i-kua-uli,*
> Come back to dwell in Hawaii-with-ridges-green,
>
> *He 'aina loa'a i ka moana,*
> A land that was formed in the ocean,
>
> *I ho'ea mai loko o ka 'ale.*
> That has risen above the waves.

The words of *mele* in the old days were characterized by the abruptness with which new ideas were introduced, by concise expressions which discarded all subordinate ideas, by a flowing poetic line, and by exquisite imagery. Not all old *mele* are easily understood. Very often there is a secondary hidden meaning, or *kaona,* describing the human emotions with figurative language and beautiful similes. In such complex poems the *kaona* tells a logical, consecutive story but the literal translation is likely to show what seem to be capricious changes of thought, causing an uninitiated person to think that the *mele* is childish and meaningless.

In the old days, the Hawaiian people had either very sensitive ears or a simple faith, for they were able to hear the songs of the tree snails on the quiet upland ridges. These tree snails are called *kahuli,* and there is a beautiful old *mele* about them which Hawaiian mothers used to sing as a lullaby. The Hawaiian words are sheer poetry:

> *Kahuli aku, kahuli mai.*
> *Kahuli lei 'ula, lei 'akolea*
> *Kolea, kolea; ki'i ka wai, wai 'akolea.*

which means:

> Trill afar, trill near.
> Kahuli with scarlet stripe, lei of 'akolea.
> Plover, plover; fetch the water
>> Water from 'Akolea (pond).

The Hawaiians believed that the words of a chant had supernatural power or *mana*, as shown by their saying, *"I ka 'olelo no ke ola, i ka 'olelo no ka make."* (In the word is life, in the word is death.) They believed that the careless change of a syllable or word which changed the meaning could offend a god, who might then mark the chanter for death. Because of this belief in the importance of the old chants, they were taught by the *haku mele* who composed them only to professional chanters called *ho'opa'a* and to dancers called *'olapa* who preserved them unchanged for centuries. Since many of the chants were sacred to a god, to an *ali'i*, or to family, they were considered to be priceless possessions, and were never revealed to strangers who might not appreciate them or who might carelessly change them. For that reason, only relatively few chants survived the coming of the white men. If you doubt that many of the educated white men who first came to Hawaii weren't properly appreciative of the unwritten literature which they heard, let's look at some proof. The following quotation is from Reverend Sheldon Dibble's 1843 "History of the Sandwich Islands":

To the heathen, the book of nature is a sealed book. The Sandwich Islands present some of the sublimest (sic) scenery on earth, but to an

*ignorant native it has no meaning.
As he looks up to the everlasting
mountains, girt with clouds and
capped with snow, he betrays no
emotion. As he climbs a towering
cliff and looks abroad on the immense rocks and mountains thrown
together by the might of God's vol-
canoes, he is thinking only of some
roots in the wilderness that may be
good for food."*

It so happens that there is a *mele* which
tells exactly what the "ignorant native"
thinks about as he looks down from a towering cliff. It is from the Legend of Pamano, and
was composed several hundred years before
Reverend Dibble wrote his indictment.

KE ONE O HULEIA

A luna au o Mahinui, As I stand on the
    heights of Mahinui
Nana ku'u maka i kai, And my eyes gaze seaward,
Me he kapa kea la i hola ia la, Like a white cloth
    that is spread out
Ke one i kai o Huleia, Is the sand below at Huleia.
I lawe ho'i au i hula, I have taken it up·as a song,
I makana 'olelo ho'i na ia la. A gift of words for her there.

UKEKE *(Stringed Bow)*
A strip of wood bent into the shape of a bow, it "... was used to accompany the mele and the oli, its chief employment was in serenading and serving the young folk in breathing their extemporized love songs and uttering their love talk—ho'oipoipo. By using a peculiar lingo or secret talk of their own invention, two lovers could hold private conversations in public and pour their loves and longings into each other's ears without fear of detection ... this display of ingenuity has been the occasion for outpouring many vials of wrath upon the sinful ukeke."
NATHANIEL B. EMERSON

Like most very old *mele,* it shows the touch of a master craftsman who composed an alliteration of pleasing sounds in a free-flowing rhythm.

There has been much controversy as to whether the Hawaiian people had melodies and used harmony before the white people came. Unfortunately, the first white persons to visit the Islands were musically untrained, so their descriptions of the ancient music are ambiguous and vague. According to the general description of travelers who had the advantage of visiting the Islands while they were practically untouched by outside influences, there was no singing as we understand the term. Instead of free, spontaneous melody which could be appreciated for its own sake, there was an intoning or chanting on two or three pitches as principal tones. The resulting melody was at best rudimentary, and though often spontaneous, tended to be monotonous.

The chants which Captain Cook heard when he first visited the Hawaiian Islands in 1778 had probably existed in that form for many generations. The first contacts of the Hawaiians with the white people caused few changes in their chants. But, in the fifty years following 1820, Hawaiian music changed from the ancient chants to a form which is substantially the same as we know today. What happened in 1820? The coming of the first missionary company in April of that year. They came to preach and teach but, since their sermons in English would have been of interest only to themselves, they held services composed largely of the singing of hymns. This was probably the first time that any large number of Hawaiian people had ever heard singing, as we understand the term, and certainly the first that any of them had ever heard four-part harmony. They were delighted by these simple songs, and came by the hundreds to hear them.

Reverend Bingham was quick to recognize the attraction music had for his new flock, and just fifty-five days after his arrival organized a singing school. Though very popular, the new singing school was not an unqualified success. Hawaiian voices, which for generations had been singing in a near monotone,

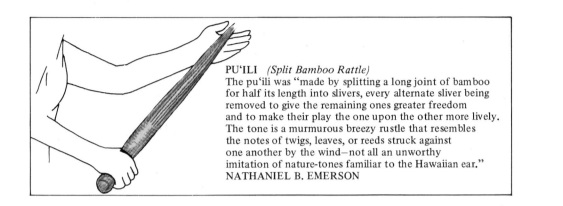

PUʻILI *(Split Bamboo Rattle)*
The puʻili was "made by splitting a long joint of bamboo
for half its length into slivers, every alternate sliver being
removed to give the remaining ones greater freedom
and to make their play the one upon the other more lively.
The tone is a murmurous breezy rustle that resembles
the notes of twigs, leaves, or reeds struck against
one another by the wind—not all an unworthy
imitation of nature-tones familiar to the Hawaiian ear."
NATHANIEL B. EMERSON

could not at once adapt to the much wider tone intervals required by the
new hymns. But adapt they did, and this was the beginning of Hawaiian
music as we know it today—a new music born of the marriage of simple
hymn tunes with the beautiful poems and exotic rhythms of ancient Hawaii.
This great interest in hymns was fortunate, for neither Reverend Bingham nor
Reverend Thurston knew enough of the Hawaiian language to be useful. Not
until the Reverend William Ellis came to Hawaii from Tahiti in 1822 did the
Hawaiians hear preaching in their own tongue. After Reverend Ellis' arrival,
books printed in the Hawaiian language were produced, and education was
eagerly sought after. The first Hawaiian hymnbook, 2,000 copies of a small
book of sixty pages with 47 hymns, came off the Mission Press in December
1823, and further stimulated learning of the written language.

The *aliʻi,* or chieftains of the Hawaiian people, composed a large percentage of the *mele* and early songs. Why were the *aliʻi* such prolific composers?
Because both their heritage and their education made them better fitted for
composition than either the *kahuna* or priests, or the *makaʻainana* or common people. In contrast to the kings of feudal Europe who were largely illit-
erate, the Hawaiian *aliʻi* were very well educated. They had a superb physical
education, and they learned the traditions of their people, the religious rites
of the *kahuna,* and many of the traditional chants. Since a large percentage
of the first arrivals in the canoes from Tahiti were *aliʻi,* a relatively large percentage of Hawaiian people are descended from *aliʻi* stock. So it is no accident that they are musical, or that the *aliʻi* composed most of the songs.

The *aliʻi* continued their composition of *mele* after the white men came.
Lord Byron, in the 1826 journal of the HMS Blonde, recorded a song by
Liholiho or King *Kamehameha II.* We know that *Kau-ike-ao-uli* or King
Kamehameha III maintained a band of native musicians, and that he spon-
sored song contests. We know too, that in 1862 *Alexander Liholiho* or King
Kamehameha IV was active in translating hymns and litanies for the Church

of England, and that the Easter service there in 1863 included the Agnus Dei and Gloria in Excelsis from Mozart's Twelfth Mass and Mendelssohn's Kyrie, all sung in Hawaiian. It is probable that *Kamehameha IV* also translated the first Christmas carols into Hawaiian.

One of the early *haku mele,* or composers, whom we know about is *Ululani,* who commemorated in verse the feat of the young *Kamehameha I* in overturning the 6,000-pound Naha Stone. In the 1860's and 1870's, four of *Ululani's* great-grandchildren were among the most talented and prolific composers in the Islands. Their names are very familiar to you: *Kalakaua, Lili'u-o-ka-lani, Likelike,* and *Lele-io-hoku.* In the late 1860's, the Hawaiian people began to form singing clubs for their own amusement, and for friendly rivalry in composing and singing new songs. This activity reached its peak during the reign of King *Kalakaua,* and the four *ali'i* just mentioned were the leaders. King *Kalakaua's* brother, Prince *Leleiohoku,* although only nineteen years old, had attracted to himself a number of convivial companions, forming a singing club which they called the *Hui Kawaihau.* They must have thought it hilariously funny to call themselves the Ice-Water Club, for it was probably the only thing they didn't drink. *Leleiohoku* was the composer of the love song *Kaua I Ka Huahua'i* which has since been perverted into the Hawaiian War Chant. His sister Princess *Lili'uokalani* also had a singing club, and in her book spoke of it in these words:

> *"There were three separate clubs engaged in friendly rivalry to outdo each other in poetry and song. Those were the friends of the Prince Regent, those of Princess Likelike, and my own friends. Candor compels me to admit that the compositions of Prince Leleiohoku were really in advance of those of his two sisters, although this was due perhaps to the fact that the singing club of*

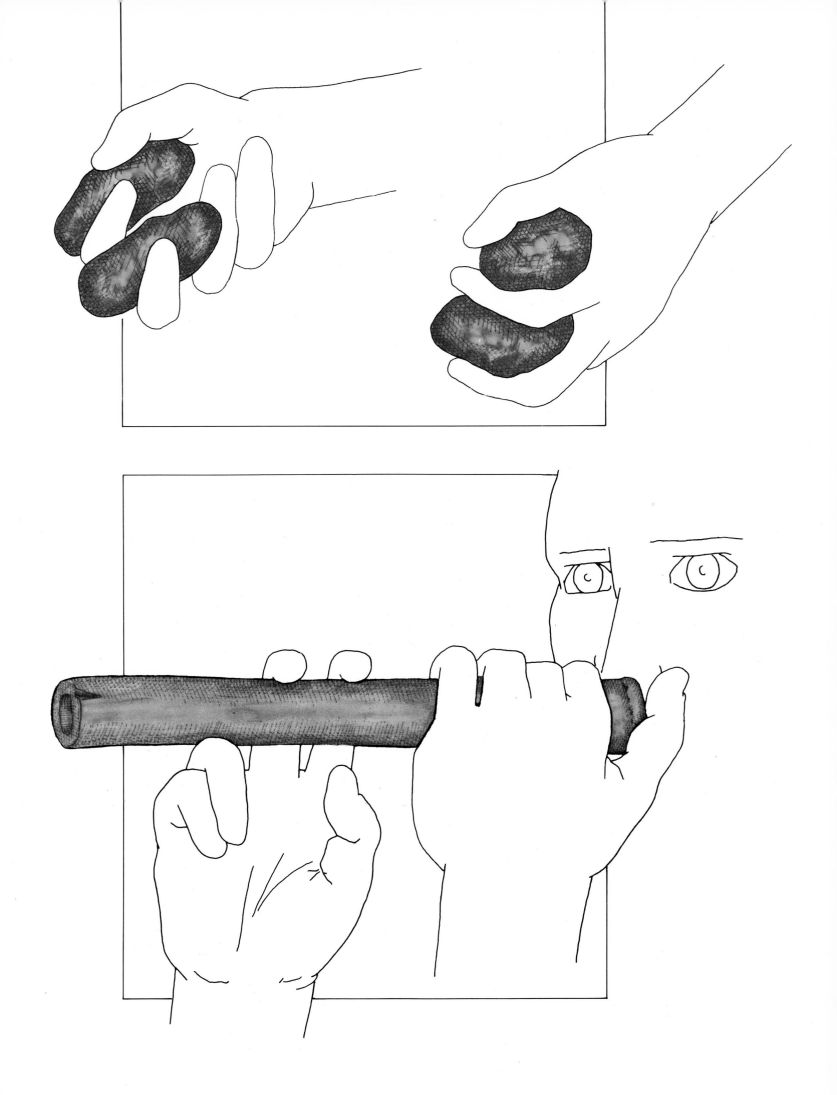

the Regent was far superior to any that we could organize. It consisted of the very purest and sweetest voices to be found amongst the native Hawaiians."

There are two songs composed by *ali'i* of that period which all of us who live in Hawaii know and sing, for they are used to open and close many public meetings. They are King *Kalakaua's* national anthem *Hawaii Pono'i* and Queen *Lili'uokalani's* beautiful *Aloha 'Oe*, both quoted here:

HAWAII PONO'I

(1)   *Hawaii pono'i, nana i kou Mo'i*
           Hawaii's own, look to your King

        Ka lani Ali'i, ke Ali'i
           The highest Chief, the Chief

(Hui)   *Makua lani e, Kamehameha e*
           The royal parent, Kamehameha

        Na kaua e pale me ka ihe.
           We shall ward with the spear.

ALOHA 'OE

(1)   *Ha'aheo e ka ua i na pali*
           Proudly the rain on the cliffs

        Ke nihi a'e la i ka nahele
           Creeps over into the forest

        E uhai ana paha i ka liko
           Swiftly swelling the buds

        Pua 'ahihi lehua o uka.
           Lehua flower of the upland.

(Hui)   *Aloha 'oe, aloha 'oe,*
           Farewell to thee, farewell to thee,

        E ke onaona noho i ka lipo.
           Fragrance dwelling in the distance.

        One fond embrace, a ho'i a'e au,
           One fond embrace, and I go

        A hui hou aku!
           Until we meet again!

The great activity of the *ali'i* in composing songs stimulated a like activity among the *maka'ainana.* It soon became fashionable and popular to compose songs. Hawaiians who for generations had been composing *mele* for every occasion now also made an appropriate tune to fit the poem. Since the *ali'i* were greatly beloved by the common people, many of their songs were dedicated to an *ali'i.* Because a song was not the property of the composer, but rather the property of the one for whom it was composed, it is sometimes very difficult to determine who actually composed a particular song.

The activity which did most to stimulate composition of music by the common people was the *ho'ike,* or exhibition, which originated as a school examination. The Reverend Hiram Bingham has described the first *ho'ike* of August 1820, in which forty scholars enthusiastically chanted in exact time the first five lines of the Book of Genesis, beginning with:

> *I kinohi hana ke Akua i ka lani a me ka honua.*
> (In the beginning God created the heaven and the earth.)

These *ho'ike* have continued to the present day, not as school examinations, but as church festivals where every spectator becomes a participant. Where everyone from a child to the eldest, contributes in his turn a song, a bit of verse, or whatever his talents permit. Many of the true Hawaiian folk songs were composed for these *ho'ike.*

One of the early *ho'ike* songs is *Iesu me ka Kanaka Waiwai* (Jesus and the Rich Man). We don't know when or by whom it was composed, but realize the thought came from Matthew 19:24, which reads: "It is easier for a camel to go through the needle's eye than for a rich man to enter into the kingdom of God." Here is the original text of this old folk song:

IESU ME KE KANAKA WAIWAI

1.   *Ma ke ala hele o Iesu*
      In the travels of Jesus

      I halawai aku ai
      He met

      Me ke kanaka opio hanohano
      With a prominent young man

      Kaulana i ka waiwai.
      Known for his wealth.

      Pane mai e ka opio:
      Said the youth:

"E ku'u Haku maika'i,
   My good Lord,

Heaha ho'i ka'u e hana aku ai
   What must I do

I loa'a e ke ola mau?"
   To have life eternal?"

(Hui)   *E ha'awi, e ha'awi lilo*
   Give, give away

I kou mau waiwai;
   Your possessions;

Huli a hahai mai ia'u,
   Turn and follow me,

I loa'a i ke ola mau ia 'oe,
   Thus have life eternal.

Some may question our calling this later Hawaiian music "folk music," in the belief that the term folk music should be reserved for songs so old that their origins are lost. Others may agree that authentic folk songs are being composed today, authentic because they have the characteristics of true folk songs. For example, much of today's Hawaiian music is unwritten, passing from person to person orally as it did in the old days. Much of it has a veiled meaning as in the old chants, with references to flowers, ferns, birds, winds, and rain instead of to persons and their actions. And much of it is stylistically similar to the old chants which had an economy of expression bordering on terseness, an emphasis on the first words of phrases, and ignored rhyme.

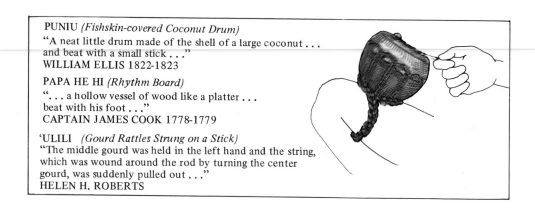

PUNIU *(Fishskin-covered Coconut Drum)*
"A neat little drum made of the shell of a large coconut . . .
and beat with a small stick . . ."
WILLIAM ELLIS 1822-1823

PAPA HE HI *(Rhythm Board)*
". . . a hollow vessel of wood like a platter . . .
beat with his foot . . ."
CAPTAIN JAMES COOK 1778-1779

'ULILI *(Gourd Rattles Strung on a Stick)*
"The middle gourd was held in the left hand and the string,
which was wound around the rod by turning the center
gourd, was suddenly pulled out . . ."
HELEN H. ROBERTS

One of the best known *ho'ike* songs is *Ekolu Mea Nui* (Three Great Things) composed for a Congregational church song contest on June 17, 1925 by Robert K. Nawahine of Maui. The song contains the words *mana'o'i'o* and *mana'olana,* excellent examples of the beautiful imagery which is inherent in the Hawaiian language. *Mana'o'i'o* means a thought which is true and dependable, an excellent description of "faith." *Mana'olana* means a thought which is buoyant and which cannot be submerged by adversity, or "hope."

There have been many other influences tending to further mould and change Hawaiian music since its earliest days. One was bandmaster Henry Berger who came to the Royal Hawaiian Band in 1872, and in the next forty-three years conducted over 30,000 band concerts, making the Hawaiian people familiar with the world's most tuneful music. But more important, it was Berger, sensitive to the beauty in the Hawaiian's adaptation of Western music, who both recognized and recorded these early songs.

The introduction of the *'ukulele* in 1879, and the development of the Hawaiian steel guitar starting in 1895 gave more prominence to the music and less to the words. Charles E. King's activities, starting about 1900, in collecting, arranging, and publishing over two hundred Hawaiian songs helped to preserve the old songs unchanged. The closing of the nineteenth century saw many composers among the common people producing a great wealth of charming song. Among them, we remember: Mekia Kealakai for *Lei 'Awapuni,* Elizabeth Doirin for *Ahi Wela,* Ernest Ka'ai for *Pu'uwa'wa'a,* Alice Everett for *'Ua Like No a Like,* Matthew Kane for *Moloka'i Nui a Hina,* Alfred Alohikea for *Hanohano Hanalei,* and David Nape for *Ku'u Ipo. Ha'ole* composers in the 1900's then contributed their share of Hawaiian songs. Where the Hawaiian composers of the 1870's had strewn English words and phrases through their songs, the *ha'ole* composers seasoned their lyrics with just enough Hawaiian words to pique the interest.

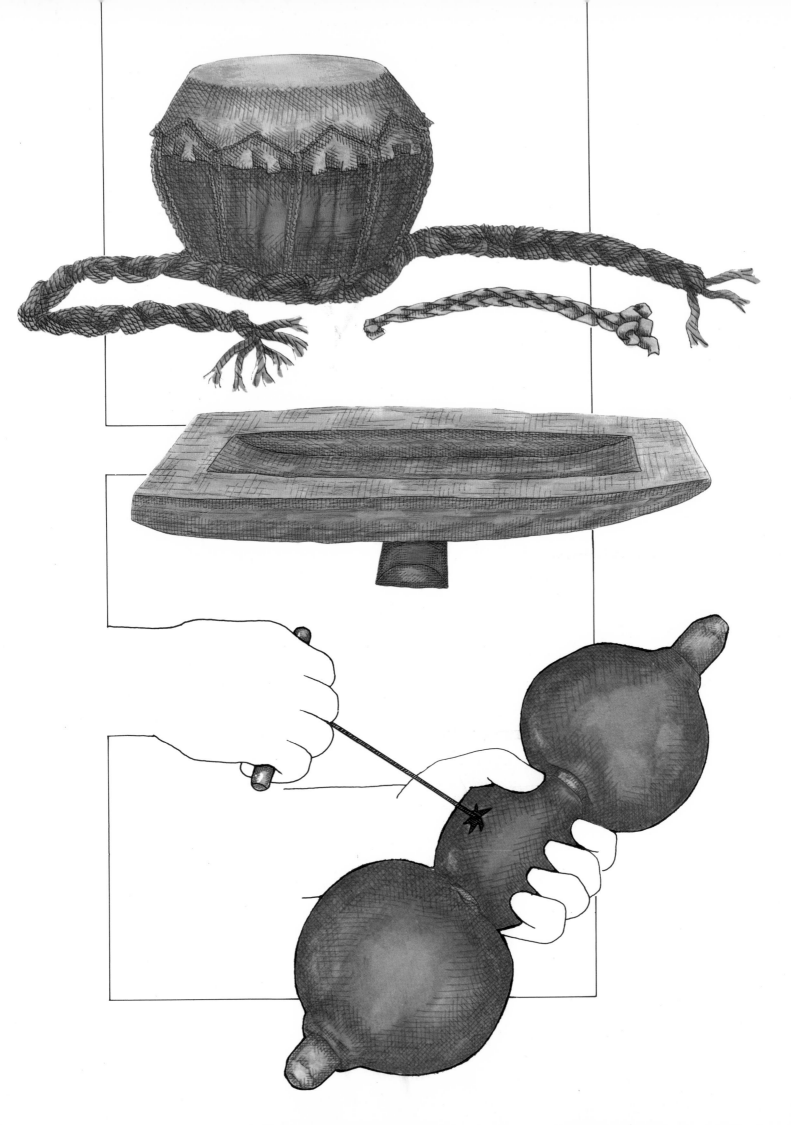

KUPE'E NIHO 'ILIO *(Dog-tooth Leg Ornament)*
"We were this day much diverted; at the beach, by the
buffooneries of one of the natives. He held in his hand an
instrument of the sort described in the last volume, some
bits of seaweed were tied round his neck; and round
each leg a piece of strong netting, about nine inches deep,
on which a great number of dog's teeth were loosely fastened
in rows. His style of dancing was entirely burlesque,
and accompanied with strange grimaces, and pantomimical
distortions of the face; which at the time inexpressibly
ridiculous, yet, on the whole, was without much
meaning or expression."
CAPTAIN JAMES KING 1778-1779

The *ho'ike* has its modern counterpart in a song contest held annually by the Board of Public Parks and Recreation, whose supervisor of music and dance, Alice Kalahui, said:

"We have had about a dozen songs for each of the Hawaiian song writing contests the Board has sponsored. The most consistent prize winners have been John K. Almeida and Mary Kawena Pukui."

From one of those song contests, we'll quote four verses of Mary Kawena Pukui's Hanauma Bay:

HANAUMA BAY

1.
    Mahalo a'e ana au
      I am admiring

    I ka nani a o Hanauma,
      The beauty of Hanauma,

    Ke kai ku'ono hala'i
      The calm bay

    Po'ai 'ia e na pali.
      Encircled by the cliffs.

3.
    He kahua na ka lehulehu
      A place for the multitude

    E luana hau'oli ai,
      To relax happily,

    E ho'olono like a'e ana
      Listening together

IPU *(Double or Single Gourd Drum)*
"Everything had been previously arranged; mats were spread in front of the cottage, and chairs were placed in a circle, and first, five singers appeared and kneeled down. Each of them armed with a large calabash, which was made thin towards the middle; this calabash, held in the left hand by a string, aided the expression of their gestures in a singular manner. They were naked to the waist; their arms and breast were tattooed, and loose folds of tapa of various colors covered the lower part of their bodies. Their songs were a sort of recitive, or of modulated conversation, animated or slow, as the subject required."
ADOLPH BARROT 1836

I ka leo hone o ke kai.
To the soft voice of the sea.

4.   *'Olu'olu i ka pe'ahi*
Cooled by gentle fanning

A ka makani aheahe,
Of the soft breeze,

E ho'ouli malie ana
Gently swaying

I na lau a o ke kiawe.
The leaves of the kiawe.

5.   *Ha'ina mai ka puana*
This is the end of my story

No ka nani a o Hanauma,
Of the beauty of Hanauma,

Ke kai ku'ono hala'i
The calm bay

Po'ai 'ia e na pali.
Encircled by the cliffs.

Although Hanauma Bay is a modern song, its theme is the same one that beguiled the *haku mele* of ancient times. It is a paean of praise for the ever-present, ever-changing wonder of nature. Praise for creamy-white surf on brilliant blue water, for sun-flecked shade under dancing kiawe leaves, for a peaceful bay nestled under encircling cliffs! Hawaiian folk music at its best!

GLOSSARY

Ahukini — A Tahitian prince, son of La'a, one of the first fathers of the Oahu and Kauai Royal Families.

'Akolea — A native fern with large lacy fronds.

Ali'i — Chief, chiefess, king, queen, noble.

Aloha — Love, affection, greeting.

Haku mele — Composer

Hala — The pandanus or screw pine, usually growing at low altitudes. The leaves were woven into mats.

Haleakala — Volcanic crater on the island of Maui. Literally, house [used] by the sun.

Hale Ola — Literally, house [of] life.

Haole — White person; formerly any foreigner.

Hapa-haole — Part-white person; part white and part Hawaiian, as an individual or phenomenon.

Hapakuela — Ancestral home of Pele and her family.

Hawai'i-loa — Legendary founder of Hawaii.

Healani — Ancestral world from which the gods and Kena came.

Hi'iaka — Younger sister of Pele who is credited with the first hula.

Hi'ilawe — Waterfall at Waipio, Hawaii. Literally, lift and carry.

Himeni — Hymn, any song not used for hulas.

Hinahina — Any of several varieties of native plants with silver green foliage.

Hina-Manouluae — Goddess of growing things. The daughter of Ku and Hina.

Ho'ihe — To show or exhibit.

Ho'oipoipo — Making love.

Honoka'a — A village at Hamakua, Hawaii. Literally, rolling (as stones) bay.

Ho'okele wa'a — Steersman, helmsman, navigator of a canoe.

Ho'opa'a — Professional chanter.

Hula — A dance, a hula dancer, to dance the hula.

'Ili'ili — Water-worn pebbles. Hula 'ili'ili, dance using pebbles.

'Ilima — Native shrubs, bearing yellow, orange, greenish or dull red flowers, much loved for leis.

Ipu hokiokio — Gourd whistle.

Ipu hula — Gourd drum used to accompany a hula.

Ka — Knee drum beater made of dried ti leaves or braided fiber.

Kahiki — Traditionally the ancient homeland of the Hawaiians. Any foreign country.

Kahuna — The ancient priest that combined knowledge of the gods with any of several professions, such as canoe building, temple construction, politics, farming, medicine, music, housebuilding, and other professional activities.

Kakuhihewa — Greatest king of Oahu.

Ka la'au — The sticks used to keep time in the stick dance. Ka, to strike; la'au, wood.

Kamalalawalu — Grandson of Piilani (traditional King of Maui), the greatest warrior prince of Maui and a king himself.

Kamapua'a — A demigod whose mother was a sea nymph and whose father was a pig, associated in legends with Pele as one of her lovers.

Kamene — One of the many lands ruled by the ancient settlers of Hawaii while enroute here. According to traditions, the lands were ruled for 511 years.

Kanaloa — One of the four major Hawaiian gods. The god of the oceans and ocean winds, with Kane, he opened springs to furnish fresh water.

Kane — One of the four major Hawaiian gods, procreator, provider of sunlight, fresh water and life substance in nature.

Kaona — Secret, hidden meaning.

Kapa — Tapa, bark cloth

Kaula — Prophet priests, greatest of all the Kahunas.

Kaulula'au — One of the princes of Molokai.

Keawe — Traditional ruling dynasty of Hawaii.

Kena — The original name of the ali'i.

Kiha — Traditional prince of Niihau.

Ko'olau — Mountain range on Oahu. Literally, windward.

Ku — One of the four major Hawaiian gods, patron of war, forest plants and protector of the nation.

Kukui — Candlenut tree, oily kernels were used for light.

Kumulipo — Ancient chant of creation.

Kupe'e niho 'ilio — Literally, bracelet or anklet of the teeth of the dog.

Kukuihaele — Village above Waipio Valley, Hawaii. Literally, traveling light referring to the night marchers seen there.

La'a — One of the Hawaiian gods of fertility, the personification of male sperm, of generation.

Laka — God of the hula.

Laupahoehoe — Town in the Hilo district of the island of Hawaii. Literally, smooth lava flat.

Lele — Honolulu is built on two plains, those of Lele and those of Mamala.

Lilinoe — Goddess of the snows, lives at Haleakala.

Lono — One of the four major Hawaiian gods. The chief god of agriculture.

Lu'au	Hawaiian feast, named for the taro tops always served.
Maka'ainana	Commoner. Literally, people that attend the land.
Makali'i	Navigator for Hawaii-loa.
Makana	Leaves of Makana, a special kind of fern found only on Kauai.
Mamala	See Lele
Mana	Supernatural or divine power.
Mano	Traditional King of Kauai, full name Mano-Ka-lanipo.
Maui	A demigod who snared the sun and discovered fire.
Mele	Song or chant.
Menehune	Believed by some to have been the original settlers of Hawaii.
Mokihana	A native tree, found only on Kauai. The small anise-scented fruits are strung in leis.
Mo'o	Lizard, or The Dragon, gods in the form of a gigantic lizard.
Ni'au kani	A rude instrument made by binding a reed of thin bamboo against a slit cut in a larger piece of bamboo. Held against the mouth it was played like a jew's harp.
'Ohe hano ihu	Literally, bamboo flute nose.
'Ohe ka'eke	Bamboo pipes played by striking on a hard surface. Literally, 'ohe, bamboo; ka, to hit, especially with a hard stroke; 'eke, sack, bag, pocket.
'Ohelo	A small shrub bearing red or yellow berries, sacred to Pele.
'Okolehao	Liquor distilled from ti root. Literally, iron bottom.
'Olapa	Dancer, now any dance accompanied by chanting and drumming on a gourd.
'Opihi	Limpet.
Pahu	Drum usually carved from the trunk of a coconut tree and occasionally from the trunk of a breadfruit tree.
Pa ipu	A gourd drum. Also the dance performed with gourd drums.
Pali	Cliff, steep hill.
Palolo	A district in Honolulu. Literally, clay.
Pana'ewa	Land division in the Hilo district, island of Hawaii. Legendary home of the mo'o destroyed by Hi'iaka, a sister of Pele.
Papa	The earth mother, mythical progenitor of the Hawaiian people.
Papa he hi	The treddle board played with ka la'au, rhythm sticks.
Pele	Goddess of the volcanoes.
Pi'ilani	Traditional King of Maui, Maui is called the fields of Piilani.
Piliaoao	The human father of Laka.
Pu	Trumpet made either from the *Charonia tritonis* or *Cassis cornuta*. Literally, blow.
Pu 'ili	A length of bamboo with one unsplit end including a node serving as handle and the other, longer split into narrow widths. It is struck against the hand or body to produce a rattling sound.
Punahele	Usually a first born child given to grandparents to be reared for future responsibilities as a family senior. A favorite.
Puniu	Small knee drum made of a coconut shell with fishskin cover.
Ti	In Hawaiian ki, a woody plant with bushy top of long shiny leaves on a slim ringed stock. Cordyline *terminalis*.
'Ukeke	A musical bow, with two or commonly three strings drawn through holes at one end. The bow is held against the mouth and the strings strummed.
'Ukulele	A small stringed instrument brought to Hawaii by the Portuguese in 1879. Literally, leaping flea.
'Ulili	A musical instrument made of three gourds pierced by a stick; a whirling sound is made by pulling a string, twirling the gourds.
'Uli'uli	A rattle made from either a gourd or the thinned out shell of a coconut. 'Uli, to rattle.
Wa	A warrior people originally from the land of Mene.
Waianae	Mountain range on Oahu. Literally, mullet water.
Waipi'o	Valley in the Hamakua district, island of Hawaii. Literally, curved water.
Wakea	The sky father, progenitor of the Hawaiian people.

BIBLIOGRAPHY

Barrot, Adolphe, *Visit of the French Sloop of War Bonite, to the Sandwich Islands, in 1836*, The Friend, Vol. 8, No. 5, Honolulu, 1850.

Beaglehole, J. C., *The Journals of Captain James Cook*, Cambridge, 1967.

Cook, Captain James and King, Captain James, *A Voyage to the Pacific Ocean*, Vols. II and III, 1785.

Ellis, William, *Journal of William Ellis*, London, 1827.

Emerson, Nathaniel B., *Unwritten Literature of Hawaii*, Rutland & Tokyo, 1965.

Luomala, Katharine, *The Menehune of Polynesia and Other Mythical People of Oceania*, B. P. Bishop Museum, Bull. 203, 1951.

Pukui, Mary K. and Elbert, Samuel H., *Hawaiian-English Dictionary*, Honolulu, 1965.

Pukui, Mary K. and Elbert, Samuel H., *Place Names of Hawaii*, Honolulu, 1966.

Te Rangi Hiroa (Buck, Peter H.), *Arts and Crafts of Hawaii*, B. P. Bishop Museum, Special Publication 45, 1957.

Roberts, Helen H., *Ancient Hawaiian Music*, Honolulu, 1926.

ACKNOWLEDGMENTS

Island Heritage would like to express its sincere appreciation to Don Tyler of Commercial Recording, Inc., Mr. Robert Lang, Mr. Hank Kuiyper of Master Color Laboratories, Harold Kaniho, Ed Bendet, Gene Lewis from Uncle Irvings, Jean Dodge of Associated Journals, Carol Jenkins, Herb and Sharon Kane, Bob Van Dorpe, Buzz and Jodi Belknap, Sammy Amalu, Robert Spicer, and Emerson C. Smith, whose counsel and assistance at various stages in this project proved invaluable. A special note of thanks to Mr. Theodore Kelsey, whose great photographs of Hawaiians, taken early in the century, are among the finest portraits we have ever seen.

Panini Productions would like to thank the following people for all their help and moral support during this project: Fellaboy Shingle, E. B. H. Siegfried, The men of 1888 J Kalakaua, Patti Keale, Alice H. Shingle, and Bob Lang.

Eddie Kamae says Mahalo Nui to: Pilahi Paki, whose kindness, guidance, and wisdom have been an inspiration; Kaupena Wong, a special friend always willing to help; Eleanor Williamson, for her help and understanding; Harold Kaniho, who flew down from Lahaina, Maui to do the donkey laugh on the recording; Irmgard Aluli for her thoughtfulness and sharing of her work; Clara Holowa'a Kailihou of Hali'imaile, Maui; the late Rev. Edward Kapoo, who shared his knowledge of Hawaiiana with me; and to the kind ladies at the church in Huelo—Hattie Apuna, Sarah Akiu, Mary Lukela.

SPONSOR

This book and the record accompanying it were made possible by the support of the Hawaii Brewing Company, Honolulu, Hawaii, makers of Primo beer. Division, Jos. Schlitz Brewing Company, Milwaukee, Wisconsin.

From all of us who love Hawaiian music, *mahalo nui* and *aloha pumehana* to Primo and the folks who make it.